Disney
Winnie the Pooh
It's Fun to Learn

The Wonders of Water

JUNE
S M T W T F S
1 2 3 4 5 6
7 8 9 10 11 12 13
14 15 16 17 18 19 20
21 22 23 24 25 26 27
28 29 30
HUNNY STORE
HUNNY

Very early one morning in the Hundred-Acre Wood, Winnie the Pooh tumbled from his bed.

"Can't be a sleepyhead this morning!" Pooh said, as he struggled to free himself from a tangle of blankets. "Today is Pooh and Piglet Paint Day!"

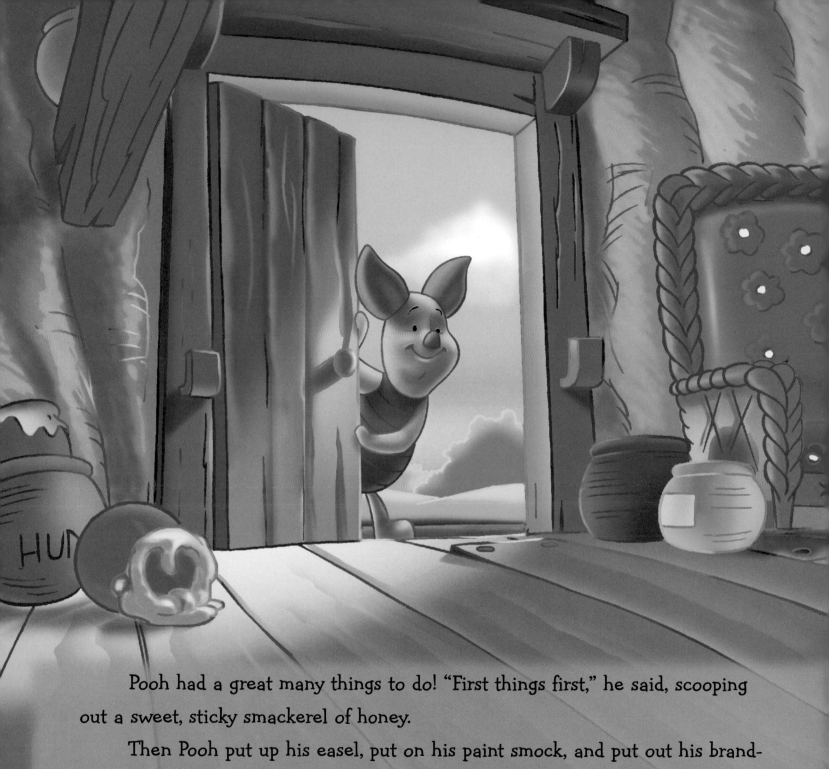

Pooh had a great many things to do! "First things first," he said, scooping
out a sweet, sticky smackerel of honey.

Then Pooh put up his easel, put on his paint smock, and put out his brand-
new watercolors.

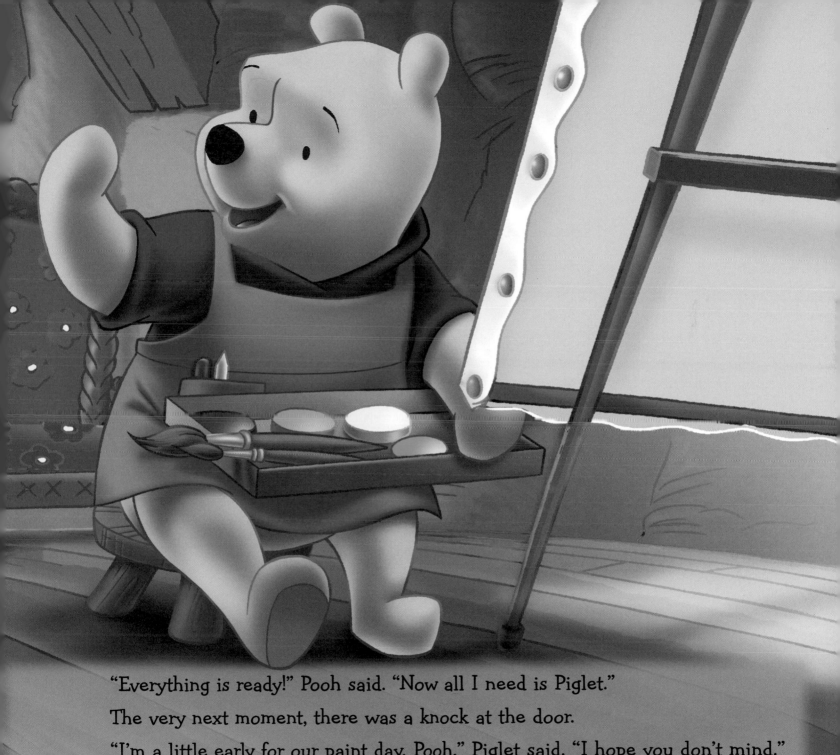

"Everything is ready!" Pooh said. "Now all I need is Piglet."

The very next moment, there was a knock at the door.

"I'm a little early for our paint day, Pooh," Piglet said. "I hope you don't mind."

"You're just in time, Piglet!" Pooh said. "Let's paint!"

Pooh and Piglet dabbed their paintbrushes into the new watercolors. But when Pooh tried to brush the color onto the paper—nothing happened!

"You try, Piglet," Pooh said. Piglet tried, but the paper stayed blank.

"Oh, bother," Pooh sighed. "I'm afraid these paints don't work."

Just then, Rabbit stopped by to drop off some carrots. "What's wrong with you?" he asked after seeing their sad faces.

"Pooh's new paints don't work," Piglet said.

"Well, of course they don't work," Rabbit said. "They're *water*colors. You need water to make watercolors work."

"Oh, is that all?" Pooh chuckled. "I can fix that."

Pooh took a bucket to the kitchen sink. But when he turned on the faucet, only a few drops of water trickled out.

"Oh, dear," said Pooh. "Nothing seems to be working today."

"Don't worry, Pooh," said Piglet. "We can get water at my sink."

The two friends walked to Piglet's house and filled the bucket. On the way back to Pooh's house, they were swinging the bucket—and they dropped it. All the water spilled out.

Pooh and Piglet sat down on the empty bucket.

Just then, Piglet noticed something sparkling on the grass.

"Look, Pooh!" he cried. "Dewdrops!"

Pooh bent to take a closer look. "Oh, yes, they're wet," noticed Pooh.

"Maybe we can use them for painting, Pooh," Piglet said.

Pooh and Piglet were trying to collect dewdrops when Owl flew up.

"I say," said Owl. "If it's water you're after, I believe there's quite a bit more of it at the stream."

"Oh, that's very good thinking, Owl," Pooh said. "We'll go there now."

On the way to the stream, Pooh and Piglet passed by Kanga and Roo's yard.
Kanga was busy washing Roo's shirts in a big tub of soapy water. Roo was busy
too—chasing bubbles.

"Want to help?" Roo called out to his friends.

"Not today," Pooh said as a bubble settled on his nose. "We're going to the stream to get water for painting."

"You can have some of this water," Roo offered.

"Soapy water is just right for cleaning, dear," Kanga smiled. "But it wouldn't do for painting with watercolors."

When Pooh and Piglet got near the stream, they heard splashing and singing. It was Tigger, playing in the water.

"Hey, Buddy Boys!" Tigger shouted. "Come on in! It's a splendiferous day for a swim!"

Tigger jumped up and down in the water, soaking Pooh and Piglet. Then he bounced out onto the stream bank—right into a huge puddle of mud!

"Want to make mud pies?" Tigger asked, wiping the mud from his face.

"No, thank you, Tigger," said Pooh politely. "We're here to get water for painting."

"This water might be a little mud-erikelous for painting," Tigger said. "The bouncier I get, the muddier it seems to get."

Tigger had an idea. "If you follow the stream that-a-way," he said, pointing, "you'll come to the pond."

"I'm pretty sure you won't find any tiggers bouncing around there," he added. "Because I'm the only tigger there is—and I'm here!"

Pooh and Piglet walked to the pond. Christopher Robin was there, sailing a toy boat.

"Isn't it splendid how it floats on the water?" he said.

"It looks like it's floating on clouds," Piglet said.

"Clouds?" Pooh cried. "In the pond?"

Pooh looked down into the water. Sure enough, he saw clouds! And then he saw a reflection of his own face!

"This water knows how to make pictures!" Pooh said.

"Yes," said Piglet. "Don't you think that makes it just perfect for painting, Pooh?"

Pooh and Piglet filled their bucket with water from the pond. They set it down—very, very gently—so they could wave good-bye to Christopher Robin. Then the two friends carefully carried the bucket back the way they had come.

When Pooh and Piglet came to the place where Tigger had been playing, it was quiet and still. Tigger was gone.

But muddy footprints and even muddier tigger-type tail prints led in the same direction Pooh and Piglet were going—toward Kanga and Roo's house.

When they got near Roo's house, Pooh and Piglet heard splashing and singing. It was Tigger, taking a bubble bath in Kanga's washtub!

"Rub-a-dub-dub, Buddy Boys!" Tigger shouted. "Watch out, or Kanga will give you a washing, too."

"They're not muddy like you," Roo laughed.

"Would you two like some lemonade?" Roo asked. "It's my mother's famous recipe. Lemons and honey—and water, of course."

"Honey—yum," Pooh said, smacking his lips.

"I put ice in it to make it extra cold," Roo said, handing a glass to each of his thirsty friends.

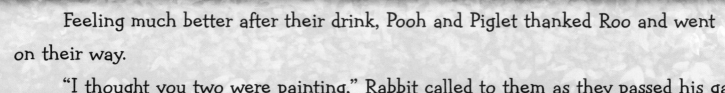

Feeling much better after their drink, Pooh and Piglet thanked Roo and went on their way.

"I thought you two were painting," Rabbit called to them as they passed his garden.

"We were. Or rather, we will be," Pooh said. "We had to get water first."

"Well, don't look at me," Rabbit said. "I need every drop of this water for my plants. If I don't water them, they don't grow. If they don't grow, I don't have vegetables to eat."

"That's okay, Rabbit," Pooh said. "We found perfect-for-painting water at the pond."

When Pooh and Piglet got back to Pooh's house, they wet their brushes and dipped them into the watercolors.

"I hope this works, Pooh," Piglet said. Then Piglet touched his brush to the paper—and painted a bright red sailboat!

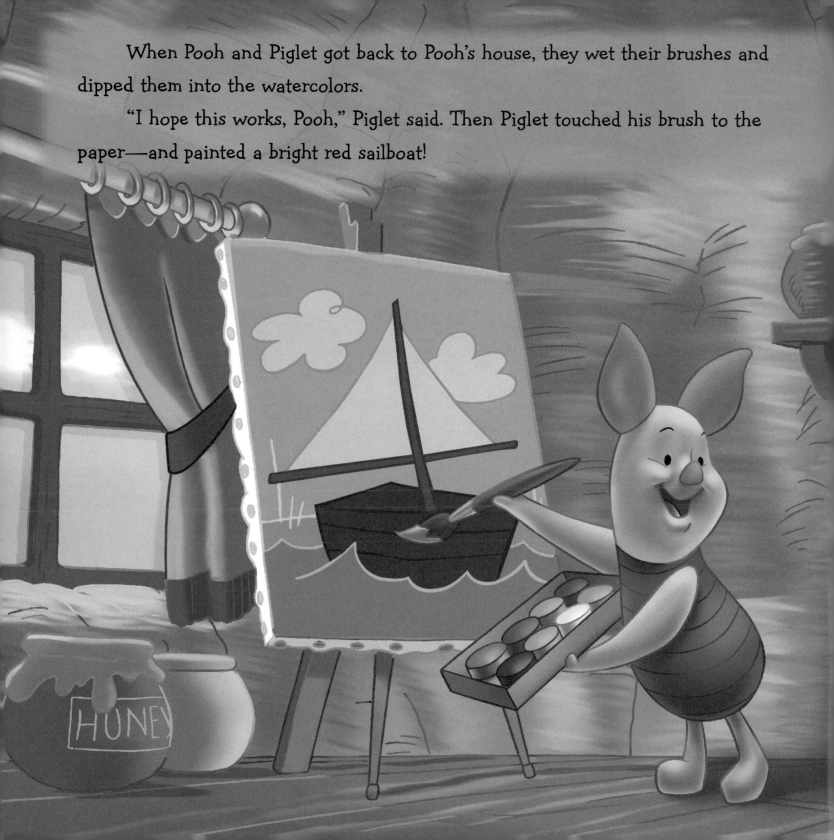

"Hooray!" Piglet cheered. He painted a blue lake under the boat.

"I think our Paint Day was a success, Pooh," Piglet said.

"Oh, yes!" said Pooh, painting a picture of a muddy brown Tigger. "A squishy, soaking, sipping, soapy, spilling, splashing success!"

Fun to Learn Activity

Hello! Splish-splash-splish! Piglet and I discovered lots of different ways to use water today. Can you go back through the story and identify all the different ways water was used?

Name the different ways that you and your family use water.